lots of
**Christmas
jokes**
for
kids

Also by Whee Winn

Lots of Jokes for Kids

Lots of Knock-Knock Jokes for Kids

The Super, Epic, Mega Joke Book for Kids

lots of Christmas jokes for kids

By Whee Winn

ZONDER**kidz**™

ZONDERKIDZ

Lots of Christmas Jokes for Kids
Copyright © 2018 by Zondervan

Requests for information should be addressed to:
Zonderkidz, 3900 Sparks Dr. SE, Grand Rapids, Michigan 49546

Library of Congress Cataloging-in-Publication Data

Names: Winn, Whee, author.
Title: Lots of Christmas jokes for kids / by Whee Winn.
Description: Grands Rapids, Michigan : Zonderkidz, [2018] |
Identifiers: LCCN 2018029996 (print) | LCCN 2018056613 (ebook) |
    ISBN 9780310767121 | ISBN 9780310767107 (paperback)
Subjects: LCSH: Wit and humor, Juvenile. | Riddles, Juvenile. | Christmas—
    Juvenile humor.
Classification: LCC PN6166 (ebook) | LCC PN6166 .W55 2018 (print) | DDC
    818/.602080334—dc23
LC record available at https://lccn.loc.gov/2018029996

Scripture quotations, unless otherwise indicated, are taken from the Holy
Bible, New International Version®, NIV®. Copyright © 1973, 1978, 1984,
2011 by Biblica, Inc.® Used by permission of Zondervan. All rights reserved
worldwide. www.Zondervan.com. The "NIV" and "New International
Version" are trademarks registered in the United States Patent and
Trademark Office by Biblica, Inc.®

Interior design: Denise Froehlich

Printed in the United States of America

---

21 22 /LSC/ 10 9 8 7 6 5 4

A Note to Jokesters

Happy Holidays!

There is not a happier and more fun-filled time of year than Christmas. Family and friends are gathering together for parties and meals. There are lots of gifts and greetings being exchanged. So what better time to break out a joke book and make the people around you laugh?

We have done all the work for you—we put together the perfect collection of holiday jokes, riddles, tongue twisters, and more so that you can entertain everyone around you. So open up this book, take a deep breath, and tell a joke.

Lots of Christmas Jokes for Kids is just the place to find good old clean and corny jokes that will have everyone around the Christmas tree snorting in the eggnog and giggling in their Christmas cookies.

A cheerful heart is good medicine.
PROVERBS 17:22

Table of Contents

1

Santa and His Helpers

What do you call Santa when he's broke?
Saint Nickel-less.

**Which of Santa's reindeer is
the most impolite?**
Rude-olph.

**How many presents can Santa
fit in an empty sack?**
Only one—after that it's not empty anymore.

What does Santa like to do in the garden?
Hoe, hoe, hoe.

**Where does Santa put his
suit after Christmas?**
In the Claus-et.

Which side of a reindeer has the most fur?
The outside.

**If eleven elves were in the workshop and
another joined them, what would he be?**
The twelf.

**Where does Santa sleep
when he's traveling?**
In a ho-ho-hotel.

Why don't you see many reindeer in zoos?
They can't afford the admission.

**What do you call someone who's afraid
of both Christmas and tight spaces?**
Santa-Claustrophobic.

Why does Santa like to go down chimneys?
Because they soot him.

Why do reindeer have fur coats?
Because they look silly in parkas.

What do you call it when Santa takes a nap?
Santa Pause.

**Why doesn't Santa get sick
from all the chimney soot?**
He got his flue shot.

Where do you find reindeer?
Depends on where you left them.

What do you call Santa after he comes down the chimney?
Cinder Claus.

What does an elf with a broken leg use to help her walk?
A candy cane.

What do you call Santa if he goes down the chimney when the fire's lit?
Crisp Kringle.

**What would a reindeer do
if she lost her tail?**
Go to a retail shop for a new one.

**What do you call a frozen elf
hanging from the ceiling?**
An elfcicle.

Why does Santa love to golf?
He always gets a ho-ho-hole in one.

How many legs do reindeer have?
Forelegs in the front and two in the back.

Knock, knock.
Who's there?
Coal.
Coal who?
Coal me if you hear Santa coming.

What did the reindeer say when he saw an elf?
Nothing—reindeer can't talk.

Why didn't the elf believe in himself?

He had low elf-esteem.

Which is Santa's favorite state?
Idaho-ho-ho.

What do you call a scary reindeer?
A cariboo.

How can you tell Santa is good at karate?
He has a black belt.

How long should a reindeer's legs be?
Just long enough to reach the ground.

**Why don't you ever see
Santa in the hospital?**
Because he has private elf care.

How do you make a slow reindeer fast?
You stop feeding it.

Where do elves go to dance?
Christmas Balls.

**What is Santa's favorite
athletic event?**
The North Pole-vault.

What did Santa name his two-legged reindeer?
Eileen.

What do you call it when Father Christmas claps his hands?
Santapplause.

What's the difference between a reindeer and a snowball?
They're both brown, except the snowball.

Knock, knock.
Who's there?
Alaska.
Alaska who?
Alaska Santa for a new bike.

**What did the elf say when
he won the lottery?**
Christmas be my lucky day.

What game do reindeer play in their stalls?
Stable tennis.

**Why did Santa get a ticket
on Christmas Eve?**
He left his sleigh in a snow parking zone.

And what happened to his sleigh?
It got mistle-towed.

**How do the elves clean the sleigh
the day after Christmas?**
They use Santa-tizer.

What goes "Oh, oh, oh"?
Santa Claus walking
backwards.

**Which reindeer can
jump higher than a house?**
All of them—houses can't jump.

What goes ho-ho-whoosh, ho-ho-whoosh?
Santa Claus stuck in a revolving door.

What do you call an elf walking backwards?
A fle.

What do you get if you cross Santa with a flying saucer?
A UF-ho-ho-ho.

Where do reindeer go to vote?
The North Poll.

What's black and white and red all over?
Santa Claus, once he's come down the chimney.

Who is an elf's favorite singer?
Elvish Presley.

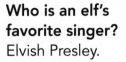

What is big and green and carries a trunk?
An elfant.

What's red and white, red and white, red and white?
Santa Claus rolling down a hill.

What did Mrs. Claus say to Santa when she saw dark clouds in the sky?
Looks like rain, dear.

What is red and white and goes up and down, up and down?
Santa in an elevator.

What do you call a rich elf?
Welfy.

What's red and white and falls down the chimney?
Santa Klutz.

What does Santa use to take pictures?
A North Pole-aroid

When should you give reindeer milk to a baby?
When it's a baby reindeer.

Knock, knock.
Who's there?
Hosanna.
Hosanna who?
Hosanna Claus going to get down our chimney?

Why doesn't the North Pole import goods?
It's elf-sufficient.

Who delivers Christmas gifts to sharks?
Santa Jaws.

Knock, knock.
Who's there?
Olive.
Olive who?
Olive the other reindeer.

Who delivers Christmas gifts to the gazelles?
Santelope.

What kind of money do elves use?
Jingle bills.

Who delivers Christmas gifts to kittens?
Santa Claws.

**What do you call a reindeer
wearing earmuffs?**
Anything—he can't hear you.

**Why did the elf push his
bed into the fireplace?**
Because he wanted to sleep like
a log.

Who delivers Christmas gifts to elephants?
Elephanta Claus.

**What do you call a
sad reindeer?**
Blue-dolph.

**Who delivers Christmas
gifts to bears?**
Panda Claus.

**What is green and
white and red all over?**
A sunburned elf.

**How did Santa win
the baseball game?**
He hit a ho-ho-home run.

What do you call a blind reindeer?
No eye deer.

What did Santa say to the elf who was making a globe in his workshop?
Small world, isn't it?

Who is married to Santa's uncle?
Auntie Claus.

What do you call a blind reindeer with no legs?
Still no eye deer.

What does Santa like to eat for breakfast?
Mistle-toast.

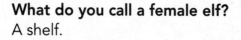

What do you call a female elf?
A shelf.

What's Santa's favorite kind of sandwich?
Peanut butter and jolly.

**What do reindeer have that
no other animals have?**
Baby reindeer.

What's Santa's favorite snack?
Crisp Pringles.

Who lives at the North Pole, makes toys, and rides around in a pumpkin?
Cinder-elf-a.

Knock, knock.
Who's there?
Sophie.
Sophie who?
Sophie good for goodness sake.

What do you call a really smart caribou?
A brain-deer.

What do you get if you cross Santa with a baby bird?

Old Saint Chick.

What's an elf's favorite sport?
Miniature golf.

What do you get if you cross Santa's home with a baby horse?
The North Foal.

What's the difference between a knight and one of Santa's reindeer?
One slays the dragon, and the other is draggin' the sleigh.

Where does Santa go swimming?
The North Pool.

Who holds Santa's books?
His books elf.

What happened when Santa Claus brought his dog to the beach?
It got sandy paws.

What is an elf's favorite track and field event?
North-pole vaulting

What do you get when you cross St. Nicholas with a detective?
Santa Clues.

Which of Santa's reindeer can fly through space?
Comet.

What do Santa's helpers learn in school?
The elf-abet.

**What kind of motorbike
does Santa ride?**
A Holly Davidson.

**What kind of music
do elves like to listen to?**
Wrap.

Santa drives a sleigh. What do elves drive?
Mini vans.

**What do you call someone who gets
emotional at Christmastime?**
Santa-mental.

If an elf drove a car, what kind would it be?
A Toy-ota.

How do you know if Santa is in the room?
You can sense his presents.

What kind of bread do elves use to make sandwiches?
Shortbread.

How much did Santa pay for his sleigh?
Nothing, it was on the house.

What is the purpose of reindeer?
It makes the grass grow, sweetie.

Why did Santa only have eight reindeer last Christmas?
Comet stayed home to clean the sink.

What do elves do after school?
Their gnome work.

What nationality is Santa Claus?
North Polish.

"I can lift a reindeer with one hand."
"I bet you can't."
"Well, find me a reindeer with one hand and I'll lift it."

Who is Santa's opposite?
Anti-Claus.

Which version of Santa is really fast?
Old Saint Quick.

What do you call a lobster who won't
share its Christmas presents?
Shellfish.

What do you call a reindeer with three eyes?
A reiiindeer.

How do you get into
Donner's house?
You ring the deer-bell.

**What did Blitzen say when he
stepped into a big puddle?**
It must have reindheer.

What smells most in a chimney?
Santa's nose.

**What is invisible but smells
like milk and cookies?**
Santa's burps.

**Why does Santa take presents to
children around the world?**
Because the presents won't take themselves.

What does Santa use when he goes fishing?
His north pole.

Where does Santa go to learn to slide down chimneys?
The chimnasium.

What's red and green and flies?
An airsick Santa Claus.

Santa's sleigh jingles too much.
He won't win the No Bell Prize.

What does Santa say at the start of a race?
Ready, set, ho, ho, ho!

What do you call a kid who doesn't believe in Christmas?
A rebel without a Claus.

Why does Scrooge love reindeer so much?
Because every single buck is dear to him.

What do you call Santa's little helpers?
Subordinate clauses.

What do you call it when Santa takes a break?
A Santa Pause.

What is Santa's favorite candy?
Jolly Ranchers.

**How did Santa describe the elf
who refused to take a bath?**
He's elfully smelly.

When does a reindeer have a trunk?
When he goes on vacation.

What was the elf allergic to?
Sh-elf-ish.

**Which one of Santa's reindeer can
be seen on Valentine's Day?**
Cupid.

**What do you get when you
cross Santa and a duck?**
Christmas quackers.

When Santa Claus sets off from the North Pole on Christmas Eve, in which direction does he travel?
South, because everywhere is south from the North Pole.

What do you call an elf who can sing and dance?
Elfish.

What is the difference between Santa's reindeer and a knight?
One is slaying dragons, and the others are draggin' the sleigh.

What did the cow say to Santa?
MOOO!

**What do reindeer have that
nothing else does?**
Baby reindeer.

2

Snow and Snowmen

Where do snowmen keep their money?
In a snowbank.

How did one snowman compliment another snowman?
You're cool.

What always falls at the North Pole but never gets hurt?
Snowflakes.

What do you get if you cross a snowman with a vampire?
Frostbite.

Who is the snowman's favorite aunt?
Aunt Arctica.

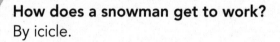

How does a snowman get to work?
By icicle.

What do you call a snowman in the summer?
A puddle.

How does a snowman lose weight?
He waits for the weather to get warmer.

Knock, knock.
Who's there?
Snow.
Snow who?
Snow use—I forgot my name again.

What's white and goes up?
A confused snowflake.

Where do snowmen go to dance?
A snowball.

What do you call a snowman on skates?
A snowmobile.

What flies when it's born, lies when it's alive, and runs when it's dead?
A snowflake.

What is a snowman's favorite food?
An iceberger.

What do snowmen eat for breakfast?
Frosted flakes.

What's a snowman's favorite snack?
Ice Krispie treats.

What does a snowman eat at a Mexican restaurant?
A brrr-ito.

What do you sing at a snowman's birthday party?
Freeze a jolly good fellow.

What bites and nips but has no teeth?
Frost.

**How do snowmen
greet each other?**
How very ice to meet you.

**What happened when the snowmen
got angry at each other?**
They gave each other the cold shoulder.

What kind of ball doesn't bounce?
A snowball.

What do snowmen wear on their heads?
Ice caps.

Why don't mountains get cold in the winter?
They wear snow-caps.

**Why was the snowman looking
through the carrots?**
He was picking his nose.

Knock, knock.
Who's there?
Scold.
Scold who?
Scold out here—let me in.

What kind of money do snowmen use?
Cold hard cash.

**What do snowmen take when
the sun gets too hot?**
A chill pill.

**What does Jack Frost like
most about school?**
Snow and tell.

**What do you call a snowman's
temper tantrum?**
A meltdown.

Why did the snowman eat a tiny pepper?
He was feeling a little chili.

**Why did the snowman have
a carrot in his nose?**
Because he forgot where the refrigerator was.

**What do snowmen like to
do on the weekend?**
Chill out.

**What do you call an
old snowman?**
Water.

**How do you know when
there is a snowman
in your bed?**
You wake up wet and
there's a carrot on your
pillow.

**What does the snowman's
wife put on her face
before she goes to bed?**
Cold cream.

What did Jack Frost say to the snowman?
Have an ice day.

First snowman: "Can you smell carrot?"
Second snowman: "No, but I can taste coal."

What do snowmen call their kids?
Chill-dren.

**What two letters of the alphabet
do snowmen prefer?**
I C

**What happened when the icicle
landed on the snowman's head?**
It knocked him out cold.

What is a snowman's favorite thing to drink?
Iced tea.

What does a snowman call his parents?
Mom and Pop-sicle.

What's ice?
Skid stuff.

What kind of cake does a snowman like?

Any kind with lots of frosting.

Knock, knock.
Who's there?
Snow.
Snow who?
Snow business like show business.

What did the police officer say when he saw a snowman stealing?
Freeze.

What does Jack Frost use to shave his face?
An ice scraper.

What is a girl snowman called?
A snow-ma'am.

Where do snowmen get the weather report?
The Winternet.

Why did the snowman turn yellow?
Ask the dog.

**What did the snowman say to
the aggressive carrot?**
Get out of my face.

Knock, knock.
Who's there?
Snowy.
Snowy who?
Snowy in the word snow, **just an S and an N
and an O and a W.**

How does Jack Frost make his bed?
With sheets of ice and blankets of snow.

Knock, knock.
Who's there?
Icy.
Icy who?
Icy you.

**What do road crews use
at the North Pole?**
Snow cones.

**What do you get when you
cross a snowman and a dog?**
Frostbite.

**Why don't mountains get
cold in the winter?**
They wear snowcaps.

**How does the snow globe feel
after a long day at work?**
A little shaken.

3

Holiday Food

Why did the Christmas turkey join the band?
He had the drumsticks.

What did the gingerbread man put on his bed?
A cookie sheet.

Who hides in a bakery at Christmas?
A mince spy.

Which Christmas carol can you hear in the produce aisle?
O Come Lettuce Adore Him.

**Why did the gingerbread man
go to see the doctor?**
He was feeling crummy.

What's the key to a great Christmas dinner?
The turkey.

Who is never hungry at Christmas dinner?
The turkey, because it's already stuffed.

Knock, knock.
Who's there?
Doughnut.
Doughnut who?
Doughnut open until Christmas.

**What happened when Humpty
Dumpty slipped on some ice?**
He bumped his egg noggin.

If fruit comes from a fruit tree, where does the Christmas turkey come from?
A poultree.

What's red and white and blue all over?
A cold candy cane.

What do herbs and spices say to each other at Christmastime?
Seasoning's greetings.

Why shouldn't you look at the turkey dressing?
Because it will make him blush.

What happened when the Christmas turkey got in a fight?
He got the stuffing knocked out of him.

Knock, knock.
Who's there?
Berry.
Berry who?
Berry Christmas.

What kind of pizza does Good King Wenceslas like best?
Deep pan, crisp and even.

What do you get if you cross a turkey with a banjo?
A turkey that can pluck itself.

**What did the grape say to
the peanut butter?**
'Tis the season to be jelly.

**What's the best thing to put in
your Christmas cookies?**
Your teeth.

"We had Grandma for Christmas dinner."
"Really? We had turkey."

**Where do Christmas trees
keep their ornaments?**
In the trunk.

What do you call a bunch of chess players bragging about their games in a hotel lobby?
Chess nuts boasting in an open foyer.

What do zombies put on their Christmas turkey?
Grave-y.

What kind of tree does a polar bear decorate for Christmas?
A fir tree.

What do you use to drain your carrots at Christmas?
An advent colander.

4

Deck
the Halls

Why are Christmas trees so bad at sewing?
They always drop their needles.

**How do Christmas trees keep
their breath fresh?**
By sucking on orna-mints.

**Where did the mistletoe go to
become rich and famous?**
Holly-wood.

Knock, knock.
Who's there?
Rabbit.
Rabbit who?
Rabbit up carefully, it's a present.

**What happens when
you put an apple on
your Christmas tree?**
It becomes a pineapple.

**What do you get if you eat your
Christmas decorations?**
Tinsellitus.

Why are Christmas trees like clumsy knitters?
They both drop their needles.

**What do Christmas trees
do instead of knitting?**
Needlepoint.

Knock, knock.
Who's there?
Arthur.
Arthur who?
Arthur any Christmas presents for me?

**What do you get when you cross
an archer and a gift-wrapper?**
Ribbon Hood.

**What do you call a
Christmas tree with
a really big nose?**
Pine-occhio.

How do fish decorate for Christmas?
They hang reefs on the door.

**What do you use to decorate
a canoe for Christmas?**
Oar-naments.

**What's the best Christmas
present in the world?**
A broken drum—you can't beat it.

Knock, knock.
Who's there?
Dexter.
Dexter who?
Dexter halls with boughs of holly.

Why do mummies like Christmas so much?
They love all the wrapping.

What did the bald man say when he got a comb for Christmas?
Thanks, I'll never part with it.

What kind of Christmas candle burns longer, a red one or a green one?
Neither—candles always burn shorter.

What did the Christmas tree say to the ornament?
Aren't you tired of hanging around?

Knock, knock.
Who's there?
Needle.
Needle who?
Needle little money for Christmas presents.

Why did Santa take his Christmas tree to the dentist?
To get a root canal.

How does a scientist decorate for Christmas?
She puts up a chemistree.

What do you call a spirit haunting your Christmas tree?
The Ghost of Christmas Presents.

**What did the big candle say
to the little candles?**
I'm going out tonight.

**Why is it getting harder to
buy Advent calendars?**
Because their days are numbered.

**What do you get if you cross a
pig with a Christmas tree?**
A porky-pine.

**How does an archer decorate
her Christmas tree?**
She puts bows on it.

**What do ducklings do to
decorate for Christmas?**
Duck the halls.

What happens if you clap for some holly?
It'll take a bough.

Knock, knock.
Who's there?
Holly.
Holly who?
Holiday greetings.

What do you put in your Christmas stocking?
Your mistle-toes.

**What do rhinos use to decorate
their Christmas trees?**
Hornaments.

Why are Christmas trees so fond of the past?
Because the present's beneath them.

**What do you call the wrapping paper
left over from opening presents?**
Christmess.

Knock, knock.
Who's there?
Yule log.
Yule log who?
**Yule log the door after you let me in, won't
you?**

What do you get when you cross an iPad with a Christmas tree?
A pineapple.

How did the ornament get addicted to Christmas?
He was hooked on trees his whole life.

Why couldn't the Christmas tree stand up?
Because Christmas trees don't have legs.

Why did the Christmas tree go to the barbershop on Christmas Eve?
He needed to get trimmed.

What do you call a Christmas tree you forget to water?
Nevergreen.

Why did the cat take so long to wrap presents?
He wouldn't stop until they were purr-fect.

Why couldn't the toys fall asleep?
They were all wound up.

5

Animals

**What happened when Santa's
cat ate a ball of yarn?**
She had mittens.

**What do you get if you cross
the Yule log with a duck?**
A fire quacker.

What do you say to a cat in December?
Mewy Christmas and happy paw-lidays.

What do fish sing during the holidays?
Christmas corals.

What's a dog's favorite Christmas carol?
Bark, the Herald Angels Sing

**Which carol is sung
in the desert?**
O Camel Ye Faithful.

**What's a monkey's
favorite Christmas song?**
Jungle Bells.

**Why did the chicken cross
the road in Paris?**
To join the other two French hens.

**How do sheep greet each
other during the holidays?**
A merry Christmas to ewe.

What does Santa give cattle for Christmas?
Cow-culators.

What do you say to an itchy Chihuahua on Christmas?
Fleas Navidad.

What do you call a chicken at the North Pole?
Lost.

What's green, covered in tinsel, and says, "Ribbet, ribbet"?
A mistle-toad.

What do you get when you cross a Christmas song with a skunk?
Jingle smells.

How do cats greet each other at Christmas?
Have a furry merry Christmas and a happy mew year.

What do you say to a bad puppy on Christmas?
Felix, naughty dog.

What do angry mice send to each other at Christmas?
Cross mouse cards.

Knock, knock.
Who's there?
Goat.
Goat who?
Goat tell it on the mountain.

What did the dentist see at the North Pole?
A molar bear.

**Why couldn't the butterfly go
to the Christmas ball?**
It was a moth ball.

**Why did the dog hang up
his stocking at Christmas?**
He was waiting for Santa Paws.

What do you call a cat on the beach at Christmastime?
Sandy Paws.

Why weren't the deer allowed into the Christmas party?
The carolers were singing, "No elk, no elk."

How does a Spanish-speaking sheep say merry Christmas?
Fleece navidad.

What do tortoises wear to keep their hands warm?
Two turtle gloves.

**What do you get if you cross
a sheep with a cicada?**
A baa humbug.

Knock, knock.
Who's there?
Dachshund.
Dachshund who?
Dachshund through the snow.

**What do you call a big, brown, jolly
animal with hooves and huge antlers?**
A merry Christmoose.

**What do you call a little bird who takes
off with your holiday decorations?**
The finch who stole Christmas.

What did the cow say on Christmas morning?
Mooooey Christmas

What does Christmas have to do with a cat lost in the desert?
They both have sandy claws.

What did the snowman call his pet cow?
Moo-ry Ann.

What did the dog breeder get when she crossed an Irish Setter with a Pointer at Christmastime?
A pointsetter.

What do you call ten rabbits hopping backwards through the snow together?
A receding hare line.

Why do Arctic seals swim in salt water?
Because pepper water makes them sneeze.

Why do birds fly South in the winter?
Because it's too far to walk.

One Christmas, Joe and Peter built a skating rink in the middle of a field. A shepherd leading his flock decided to take a shortcut across the rink. The sheep, however, were afraid of the ice and wouldn't cross it. Desperate, the shepherd began tugging them to the other side. "Look at that," remarked Peter to Joe. "That guy is trying to pull the wool over our ice."

What is twenty feet tall, has sharp teeth, and goes "Ho Ho Ho"?
Tyranno-santa Rex.

What do you get when you cross a snowman with a polar bear?
A brr-grr.

How does a mouse get around during the winter?
Mice skates.

What do sheep say to shepherds at Christmastime?
Season's Bleatings.

What is a bird's favorite Christmas story?
The Finch Who Stole Christmas.

**What do you call an amphibian
hanging from the ceiling?**
Mistletoad.

Why do reindeer have the best stories?
They always carry a tail with them.

**What do you get when you
cross a bell with a skunk?**
Jingle smells.

What squeaks and is scary?
The Ghost of Christmouse Past.

What animal loves to go downhill in the snow?
A mo-ski-toe.

6

Knock-Knock Jokes

Knock, knock.
Who's there?
Gladys.
Gladys who?
Gladys finally Christmastime.

Knock, knock.
Who's there?
Frankie.
Frankie who?
Frankie-cense, gold, and myrrh.

Knock, knock.
Who's there?
Andy.
Andy who?
Andy partridge in a pear tree.

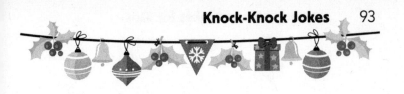

Knock, knock.
Who's there?
Harold.
Harold who?
Harold angels sing, "Glory to the newborn king."

Knock, knock.
Who's there?
Mary and Abby.
Mary and Abby who?
Mary Christmas and an Abby New Year.

Knock, knock.
Who's there?
Irish.
Irish who?
Irish you a merry Christmas.

Knock, knock.
Who's there?
Joaquin.
Joaquin who?
Joaquin in a winter wonderland.

Knock, knock.
Who's there?
Allie.
Allie who?
Allie want for Christmas is you.

Knock, knock.
Who's there?
Avery.
Avery who?
Avery merry Christmas to you.

Knock, knock.
Who's there?
Mayor.
Mayor who?
**Mayor days be merry
and bright.**

Knock Knock.
Who's there?
Lettuce.
Lettuce who?
Lettuce in, it's freezing outside.

Knock, knock.
Who's there?
Murray.
Murray who?
Murray Christmas to one and all!

Knock, knock.
Who's there?
Pizza.
Pizza,who?
Pizza the earth, good will toward men!

Knock, knock.
Who's there?
Dewey.
Dewey who?
Dewey know how long until Santa gets here?

Knock, knock.
Who's there?
Honda.
Honda who?
Honda first day of Christmas, my true love sent to me ...

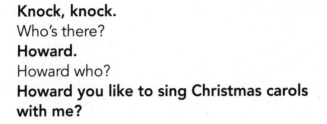

Knock, knock.
Who's there?
Howard.
Howard who?
Howard you like to sing Christmas carols with me?

Knock, knock.
Who's there?
Holly.
Holly who?
Holly-days are here again.

Knock, knock.
Who's there?
Snow.
Snow who?
Snow one's at the door.

Knock, knock.
Who's there?
Yule.
Yule who?
Yule know when you answer the door.

7

Bonus Jokes

Why are there only 25 letters in the alphabet on Christmas?
There's no L.

What did Adam say the day before Christmas?
It's Christmas, Eve.

Why is it so cold at Christmastime?
Because it's Decembrrr.

When does Christmas come before Thanksgiving?
In the dictionary.

What's a vampire's favorite Christmas song?
I'm Dreaming of a Bite Christmas.

**What do you call a
trio of tiny magi?**
Wee three kings.

**How did Scrooge win
the football game?**
The Ghost of Christmas
passed.

**How much difference is
there between the North
Pole and the South Pole?**
All the difference in the
world.

**Why would you invite a mushroom
to a Christmas party?**
He's a fungi to be with.

**What Christmas carol do you get if you put
a very quiet person in a suit of armor?**
Silent Knight.

**What did Dracula say at the
Christmas party?**
Fancy a bite?

Why is everyone thirsty at the North Pole?
No well, no well.

**What happened to the thief who
stole a Christmas calendar?**
He got 12 months

What's in December that's not in any of the other months?
The letter D.

Why didn't the Ghost of Christmas Past go to the party?
He had no body to go with.

Why is a can in a Christmas hat like someone from the United States?
They're both a merry can.

Which carol do you get if you cross Swiss cheese with a suit of armor?
O Holey Knight.

**How did Mary and Joseph know
how heavy Baby Jesus was?**
They had a weigh in a manger.

What comes at the end of Christmas Day?
The letter Y.

**What song did the guests sing
at the Elf Christmas party?**
Freeze a jolly fellow

**What do hip-hop artists
do on Christmas?**
Unwrap

What is a parent's favorite Christmas carol?
Silent night.

**What should you give your
parents at Christmas?**
A list of what you want.

**What's the difference between the Christmas
alphabet and the regular alphabet?**
The Christmas alphabet has Noel.

**In what year did Christmas Day and
New Year's Day fall in the same year?**
It happens every year—one's at the beginning
and one's at the end.

What's a good holiday tip?
Never catch snowflakes with your tongue if
you see birds flying south for the winter.

What did the ghost say to Santa Claus?
I'll have a boo Christmas without you.

When are your eyes not eyes?
When the winter wind makes them water.

**What did the big furry hat say
to the warm woolly scarf?**
You hang around while I go on ahead.

Knock, knock.
Who's there?
Emma.
Emma who?
Emma bit cold out here—let me in.

What is Sherlock's favorite Christmas song?
"I'll be Holmes for Christmas"

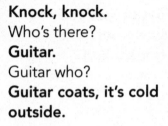

Knock, knock.
Who's there?
Guitar.
Guitar who?
Guitar coats, it's cold outside.

It was Christmas and the judge was in a merry mood as he asked the prisoner, "What are you charged with?"
"Doing my Christmas shopping early," replied the defendant.
"That's no offense," said the judge. "How early were you doing this shopping?"
"Before the store opened."

What do you call a slow skier?
A slopepoke.

If I'm standing at the North Pole, facing the South Pole, and the East is on my left hand, what's on my right hand?
Fingers.

What did the stamp say to the Christmas card?
Stick with me and we'll go places.

**What does the Grinch do
with a baseball bat?**
Hits a gnome and runs.

**What part of the body do you
only see around Christmas?**
The mistletoe.

**What does Tarzan sing
at Christmas?**
Jungle Bells.

8

Tongue Twisters

Seven Santas sang silly songs.

Tiny Timmy trims tall trees with tinsel.

Santa's sleigh slides on slick snow.

Bobby brings bright bells.

How many deer would a reindeer reign if a reindeer could reign deer?

Running reindeer romp 'round red wreaths.

Kris Kringle chose to climb the chimney at Christmas.

Chilly chipper children cheerfully chant.

Two trains travel together to Toyland.

Eleven elves licked eleven little licorice lollipops.

Ten tiny tin trains toot ten times.

Santa stuffs Steph's striped stocking.

There's chimney soot on Santa's suit.

Comet cuddles cute Christmas kittens carefully.

Hollie hangs holly hoping happy holidays hurry.

Silly Santa silently sleeps safely on the sleigh.

Kris Kringle clapped crisply.

Paul's presents present particular problems placed parallel to pink poinsettias.

Tree trimmers try to trim trees while Tracy tastes treats.

Wrapping warped wreaths risks ruining weather-wilted wood.

Youthful yeoman yodel yule yarns while yachting.

Santa seems seriously sick since Sally served sour salmon soup.

Reindeer run rings round Rover.

Santa's seven sleighs slide sideways.

The silly smelly snowman slips and slides.

Crazy kids clamor for candy canes and Christmas cookies.

Bobby bobbles a billion brilliant bells.

Hal had happy holiday holly.

Kris Kringle crunches candy canes.

Prancer presents pumpkin pies and presents.

Pretty packages perfectly packed in paper.

Santa secretly sips sugary syrup.

Ten tiny toy soldiers tinker with twenty toy trains.

Candy cane cookies keep kids coming.

Chocolate cocoa cravings cure colds.

Mrs. Claus counted Christmas carolers.

Comet caught a cold on Christmas.

Harry hung holly on the hearth for the holidays.

Clever Carol carries crimson candles carefully.

Roy bought toy boats.

Santa's sack sags slightly.

Snow slows Santa's sleigh.

Eight elves elegantly ate everything.

Blitzen bobbles a billion brilliant bells.

Santa's short suit shrank.

Lots of Jokes for Kids

Q: What do you get when you cross a parrot and a centipede?

A: A walkie-talkie!

Q: What kind of light did Noah install on the ark?

A: Floodlights

Introducing a collection of jokes that's hilarious, clean, and kid-friendly and includes everything from knock-knock jokes to Q&A jokes, tongue twisters, and a whole lot more. *Lots of Jokes for Kids* is certain to have every kid you know laughing out loud, snorting riotously, and generally gasping for air.

Lots of Knock-Knock Jokes for Kids

Whee Winn

Includes Over 250 Jokes!

Knock, knock.
Who's there?
Woo.
Woo who?
Don't get so excited, it's just a joke!

Knock, knock.
Who's there?
Anita.
Anita who?
Anita borrow a pencil.

New from Zonderkidz, here's a collection of knock-knock jokes that is both hilarious and wholesome. *Lots of Knock-Knock Jokes for Kids* is sure to send every kid you know to his knees in a breath-stealing, side-splitting, uncontrollable fit of giggles. It's that funny. And with more than 350 jokes, the laughs are sure to never quit.

This collection provides fun for the whole family and includes bonus Q& A jokes and riddles too!

Available in stores and online!

ZONDER**kidz**™

Super, Epic, Mega Joke Book for Kids

Whee Winn

The Super, Epic, Mega, Joke Book is just the thing for comedians and joke-lovers, young and old! Kid-friendly and fun, this collection of hundreds of jokes, riddles, tongue twisters, and more will keep everyone giggling for hours.

So, what's the funniest joke you'll find in this book?

Knock, knock.

Who's there?

Lena.

Lena who?

Lena little closer and I'll tell you!